YOU ARE MAGIC

Dr. Seema Ashutosh Singh

First Published in 2020

Becomeshakespeare.com

One Point Six Technologies Pvt Ltd

123, Building J2, Shram Seva Premises,
Wadala Truck Depot, Wadala (East),
Mumbai 400037, India

T: +91 8080226699

Wordit Art Fund helps deserving authors publish their work by providing monetary support. To apply for funding, please visit us at www.BecomeShakespeare.com

ISBN - 978-93-90543-66-3

Dedicated
To my Parents
Shanti Singh Kislaya & Hareram Singh Kislaya

Preface

"Out of your Strength"

- Sigmund Freud

"An idea can change your life" was the tagline of a cellular company which I came across very often during my struggling days. 'What is that idea?', 'Where can I get that idea?', 'Who can give me that idea?', 'Is there anything else then ideas which can change 'my' life?' and 'What it takes to be successful?' etc., were few questions I used to ponder over in my quest of finding the ultimate success in my life. However, I never knew that the answers to these questions lied 'within' me. 'I' was the way-out to this labyrinth path of success.

'You are Magic' is that 'IDEA' which can change anyone's life. The self-realisation, knowing oneself inside-out, realisation of innate qualities and potentials are most precious resource one has to his / her disposal. By harnessing these resources and channelizing them in the right direction, it can take you wherever you aspire to be in your life.

The author has greatly inspired many individuals with her rich experience and guidance before becoming a best-selling author herself. Following up on the her collective wisdom and life changing principles of Self-Realisation, the book provides simple, practical and most importantly workable applications for bringing out the best out of oneself for enhancing life and achieving success.

The only purpose to present these thoughts in a book form was to provide the reader with an absolutely new sense of approach towards life, free from the earlier orthodox one of believing in luck, time, stars and planets and to create a new concept and approach to take up any challenge by sheer hard work and the will to achieve success. Any challenge, however difficult, can be overcome by strong attitude of commitment but if we become slack in our efforts, then nobody is likely to come to our rescue.

This book deals with important aspects of an individual's life such as Goals, Success, Positive and Negative attitudes. It also helps in understanding the path and road of achieving success and ultimately the goal. It describes the way of achieving one's goal on one hand and on the other talks about the importance of failure and mistakes. It is very truly said that one learns from past failures and mistakes.

The author also mentions reasons about why some succeed and other fail and how one should approach both situations. The book would help a lot of readers in achieving what they want to and also try removing negative aspects that they have within.

The book discusses about the preparation required behind success. The principles enumerated in the book are backed by the success stories of Steve Jobs, Larry Page & Sergey Brin and such likes. It also helps in finding out ways and means to cope up with Change, importance of Adaptability in adverse conditions and managing challenges posed in the path.

This book is to be read with an action plan. The Reader-Author team must decide and prepare with the following objects:

- (a) Identification and fixing of goal?
- (b) Listing out our strength and weakness.
- (c) Removal of slackness or weakness in our efforts or thoughts.
- (d) Working on modification of approach as suggested in the book.
- (e) Marking progress.

We always need to bear in mind that if our direction is right and dedication earnest, then there can absolutely be no reason for any failure in achieving our goals.

A thorough reading of this book shall lead you out of the darkness of despair and into the light of a successful life and you'll discover that **you** too, have the ability to create a **MAGIC.**

Wishing a successful life

Dr. Seema Ashutosh Singh

Acknowledgement

At the outset I am grateful to THE ALMIGHTY who gave the strength to my wings for embarking on this new journey.

The very thought of writing a book on the subject was instilled in me by my father *Shri Hareram Singh Kislaya* who has been my guide, philosopher, friend and supported me through thick and thins and always believed in me. My thoughts were further propelled by my life companion *Ashutosh Singh* who has been the fuel of the fire radiating inside me and inspired me to walk on a road less travelled. Without their encouragement, undeterred support and sacrifices, the publication of this book would not have been possible.

Also as an educator, it was incumbent upon me to give back to the society whatever little I had acquired through my experience (read 'lessons of life' or 'mistakes' to be precise) and the research work with others to bring about the change we all would like to see in our life.

I wish to place on record the contributions of the scholars, educationists, administrators, educational entrepreneurs and top leadership of prestigious institutions in India and overseas whom I had met during the process of writing this book or otherwise and came across their views on the system and the ideas of future they oversee. I went through many of their path-breaking works in the field of academics, educational psychology, educational technology and management & leadership.

I am especially thankful to my colleagues, fellow scholars and researchers who were kind enough, generous and above all patient for having hours of brainstorming sessions which churned our oceanic and boundless minds to bring out nectar and other boons as well. Their ideas and research work helped immensely to shape up this book.

I am highly indebted to all my professors who taught me and provided enough knowledge and a broader perspective to frame this book with wider objectives. I am also thankful to those numerous authors of various books and journals whose great mastery work I have consulted during the preparation of various chapters of the book.

I would like to express my gratitude to the Editor of this book for going through patiently the manuscript and bearing with me and my writing skills and providing valuable suggestions for making the book more readable. I express my grateful appreciation to those who directly and indirectly helped, supported and guided me in preparation of this book.

My special thanks to the publisher of this book for bridging the gap between me and my readers and bestowing me with the opportunity to interact with them.

In the end I would like to acknowledge my son Achintya and daughter Ayannaa for believing in me and helping me in spreading the magic of words.

I do not delude into thinking that my views are final. If by any chance it finds its way into scholarly hands and invest their thoughtful attention, I shall feel pleased to be told as to how to rehash my interpretations.

Happy readings ☺

Dr. Seema Ashutosh Singh

Contents

CHAPTER 6

CHAPTER 7

CHAPTER 8

CHAPTER 9

CHAPTER 10

CHAPTER 11

CHAPTER 12

CHAPTER 13

कर्मण्येवाधिकारस्ते मा फलेषु कदाचन ।
मा कर्मफलहेतुर्भुर्मा ते संगोऽस्त्वकर्मणि ॥

During, the Epic War of Mahabharata when Arjun was not willing to fight as people standing opposite of him were the ones he considers his own. Arjun asks Krishna, "What's the use of fighting against my own for just a piece of land". What happiness will I get by slaying my dear ones? The ones on the other side are my own uncle and cousins. Won't I be committing a sin? What will I get by killing all of them? Instead, I would have preferred that they kill me here itself. To this Lord Krishna said to Arjun that "Your right is to perform your duties and not worry about the results, but never to the results. Never be motivated by the results of your actions, nor should you be emotionally involved while performing your prescribed duties."

Introduction

"*Success* is peace of mind, which is a direct result of self-satisfaction in knowing you made the effort to do your best to become the best that you are capable of becoming." – John Wooden

1. Are 'winning' and 'success' synonyms to each other; or are they a different ball game altogether. Actually success is more about the journey than the outcome and the efforts you put into achieving your goals is more rewarding both psychological and physical.

2. All humans on the Earth strive to be successful in all of their endeavours. Maslow in his "Theory of Motivation" suggests that once the basic needs of human beings are satisfied in the Hierarchy of Needs, then all their activities will be directed towards meeting the set of needs that are yet to be satisfied which desire to be in the order of hierarchy like for Self-Esteem, Self-Praise, and respect in the society.

3. Every person is capable and has a desire to move up the hierarchy toward a level of self-actualization. Unfortunately, progress is often

disrupted by a failure to meet lower level needs. Life experiences, including divorce and loss of a job may cause an individual to fluctuate between levels of the hierarchy. Therefore, not everyone will move through the hierarchy in a uni-directional manner but may move back and forth between the different types of needs.

4. Struggles, difficulties, failures are faced by everyone in this world, no one can say that they have been living a struggle free life or they haven't faced any failures yet. Many think or many people have a myth that successful people become rich and successful because of their luck and they don't face any failure or bad times. Every individual in this world face problems and failures, but the only difference between successful people and normal people is that they never give up until and unless they don't achieve what they always dreament about.

5. People become successful when they have strength and courage to stand up after falling and move on vigorously with the same vision which they had in their mind about their goals, as it says, "Falling down is an accident but staying down is a choice"

6. And successful people never remain down they move on in order to achieve their dreams and goals. Today, I will share India's few successful people's list who failed/struggled but didn't give up and finally achieved their dream life and became successful. Struggle makes you strong, failure gives you experience. Get up and move on with the same determination, efforts and attitude.

Below, here I am providing some great and successful people's wise words

PURSUE YOUR GOALS EVEN IN THE FACE OF DIFFICULTIES AND CONVERT ADVERSITIES INTO OPPORTUNITIES.

- Dhiru Bhai Ambani

THAT WHICH LAST LONG IS NOT EASILY GOT, THAT WHICH EASILY GOT, DOES NOT LAST LONG.

- Amitabh Bachchan

IF YOU ARE BORN POOR IT'S NOT YOUR MISTAKE BUT IF YOU DIE POOR IT'S YOUR MISTAKE.

- Bill Gates

Tips to a Successful Life

1. In this world of ever growing competition and the race for reaching heights of success in life, it has been the first and foremost ambition of each constituent of our Society to look for ways to achieve goals in a short span of time but also to reach them substantially .

2. While embroiled in our day to day problems and those innumerable nit-bits which are part of it, we spend our energy in always dreaming about those ambitions and making audacious plans.

3. We are hardly active and energetic enough to achieve those dreams which, although are unbelievable and are always within one's reach albeit with

    (a) Self-Confidence

    (b) Positive Approach

    (c) Self-Belief

    (d) Self-Motivation

    (e) Physical Fitness

    (f) Follow your inner voice

(g) Self- Discipline.

4. Completion of any job in itself does not constitute success. Rather the steps taken to achieve such completion have their individual importance. Perpetual small steps taken in the right direction with conviction and determination, fighting against all odds by imbibing the above said principles in your life, one can still reach to audacious heights and taste the nectar called SUCCESS.

> **"Your success will be determined by your own confidence and fortitude."**

Chapter 1

Preparing yourself for Success: Self Confidence

1. Everyone admires a self-confident person. We may even envy them a little! Self-confident people seem to be at ease with themselves and their work. They invite trust and inspire confidence in others. They are attractive characteristics. It's not always easy to be confident in yourself, particularly if you're naturally self-critical, or if other people look down upon you. But there are steps that you can take to increase and maintain your self-confidence.

2. Self-confidence is an understanding that you trust your own judgement and abilities, and that you value yourself and feel worthy, regardless of any imperfections or what others may think about you. Self-efficiency and self-esteem are sometimes used interchangeably with self-confidence, but they are subtly

different. We gain a sense of self-efficiency when we see ourselves (and other like us) mastering skills and achieving goals. This encourages us to believe that, if we learn and work hard in a particular are, we'll succeed. It's this type of confidence that leads people to accept difficult challenges and to keep going in face of setbacks.

3. If you want to be happy and a successful person, it is so important to keep believing in yourself and remain self-confident. What you need for this? Just be faithful to yourself and your own values, always do your best and don't try to avoid mistakes, as we can learn more from our failures then from our achievements.

4. The most important step in building self-confidence is simply to take action. *Inaction breeds doubt and fear. Action breeds confidence and courage. If you want to conquer fear, do not sit at home and think about it. Go out and get busy. Nothing builds self-esteem and self-confidence like accomplishments. Having once decided to achieve a certain task, achieve it at all costs of tedium and distaste. The gain in self-confidence of having accomplished a tiresome labour is immense.*

5. Nobody is born with limitless self-confidence. If someone seems to have incredible self-confident it's because he or she has worked on building it for years. Self-confidence is something that you learn to build up because the competitive world and life in general, can deflate it. The key is to be persistent and to find the ways to improve your confidence so you can be successful in life. Here are few suggestions to increase your self-confidence and self-esteem in your life.

Analyze Your Weaknesses and Strengths: It is indeed necessary to know what you are good at. Once you realize your skill sets, the next step is to focus on those things that you are good at doing. It is not possible that a person is good at everything so don't belittle yourself.

Self-Acceptance: Accepting yourself is a big step, but it is the most important one of your life. You are unique in this world. It is important that you do not beat yourself up over the things that you have trouble doing. Instead of complaining about what your weaknesses are, try to find ways to improve your life. It is preferable to develop skills by enrolling yourself in a course of instructions.

Cherish Your Successes: Many people downplay their successes and focus on those things they struggle with. This is one of the worst things you are doing to yourself.

Always remind yourself of your past accomplishments no matter how small they may be. Do not downplay the positive parts of your life. Stop focusing on the negative parts of your life and instead concentrate on your past achievements.

Positive Affirmations: There will be moments of failure. One may feel low and decide to quit. To overcome these read positive affirmations that make you feel confident daily. Read a self-help book and then write down all of the things that motivate you. It will be a bad idea to focus on the things that make you feel anxious and fearful.

Where do you see yourself? It is impossible to reach anywhere without planning. So take time to think about your expectations from life as it provides clarity. It helps to reduce the overall vision into actions which are essential to translate plan to execution.

Set Goals: Set realistic and achievable goals on a regular basis and then take small steps to accomplish them. Make sure to review progress and put all your efforts to achieve the target. Don't get upset if you don't accomplish all of your goals. You can always change your goals so that you can be more successful.

Be Persistent: Do not give up in achieving your goals in your life. Learn from your mistakes and try to improve on your situation. Do not make excuses on why you should quit or give up. Sometimes it takes a lot of effort to be successful. The key is to keep at it until you get what you want.

Face your fears: Do one thing that scares you every day. You gain strength, courage and confidence by every experience in which you will really stop looking with fear in the face. You are able to say to yourself, 'I have lived through this horror. I can take the next thing that comes along.' You must do the thing you think you cannot do.

Question your inner critic: Your inner-critic is the biggest impediment in building of your self-confidence. Don't let your inner critic question your self-worth for you are theory yet to formulate. You don't have to do anything especially worthy to build or deserve self-esteem; all you have to do is turn off that critical, haranguing inner voice.

Care for yourself: Make time to cultivate great habits of exercising, eating and sleeping. In addition, dress the way you want to feel. You have heard the saying that "Clothes make the man". Build your self-confidence by making the effort to look after your own needs.

Chapter 2

Preparing yourself for Success: Positive Approach

**"Achieving something with Negative approach and getting it, is called 'Luck'. Achieving something with
Positive approach and getting it, is called Success"**

1. Is your glass half-empty or half-full? How you answer this age-old question about positive thinking may reflect your outlook on life, your attitude toward yourself, and whether you're optimistic or pessimistic

2. Positive thinking is an attitude that pushes you to expect good and desired results. Power of positivity helps you in creating and transforming energy into reality. Positive mindset helps you to seek happiness, health and a happy ending regardless of the situation.

3. Lots of successful people have recognized the positivity as the key to success. Power of positivity may change your personal and professional life. Thus, in the tough situations, people ask you to think positive. Now you may have keenness to know what makes positivity a must for you to meet success. So, let's learn some benefits of positive thinking.

4. **Benefits of Positive Thinking.**

    (a) **It keeps Stress at Bay:** Always remember, most of your stress comes from how you react to a problem and not the problem itself. Adjust your attitude first and then tackle the problem stress free. There will be endless moments of negative thoughts due to personal or professional reasons. Believing in power of positivity can help you in avoiding stress. Positive approach will turn these adversities into opportunities. Stress is going to be only a hindrance in your path of success.

    (b) **Helps to lead a Happy and Healthy Life.** Positive approach helps with stress management thus can improve one's physical and mental health. It increases the life span, lowers the rate of depression and distress, increases the level of resistance to common cold, gives better psychological and physical well-being along with better cardiovascular health that helps in the reduction of deaths from disease caused by it and also assist in better coping skills during hardships and times of stress.

(c) **Builds Confidence and Self-Esteem:** Positive approach helps you to know yourself better and allows you to harness your abilities optimally and in an effective and efficient manner. Power of positivity promotes confidence. It boosts your self-Esteem as you work independently believing in your skills. Positive thoughts keep you always motivated in life.

(d) **Improves Decision-Making Abilities**: Under stress and tense phase of life people often make bad decisions and regret thereafter. Tension or stress reduces your power of thinking. It hastens you to make a decision. On the other hand, a positive thinker may find it easy to make decisions. He or she can give the right amount of thought to the situation at hand. It is the key to success for a positive thinker.

(e) **It Leads to Success:** The power of positivity helps you in discovering your skills. You can find the ray of hope in the darkest of hours with a positive mindset. All of these are essentials to reach success. Optimism also helps you to meet joy. It makes your personality appealing to the people. This way you can help other people change the way of their thinking. Furthermore, you can also learn much from them.

5. **Positive Thinking Techniques.**

(a) **Encourage Positivity at the Start of the Day**: At times, you may encounter something unfavorable in the morning. This undesired thing may instill bad thoughts in your mind. These thoughts may carry with you all day. As a result, you may keep thinking negative all day. Encouraging positive thoughts is the key to success in such situation. You must make yourself remember that negative thoughts are not helpful. It will help you in having a positive day.

(b) **Focus on the Good Things and Try Humour:** Difficulties and life run parallel. Sometimes in the day, you may have some problems in attempting your academic tasks. Or you may have some other personal issues. In such situation, you must focus on the things that seem pleasing. For example, if writing a section of the assignment seems difficult to you, then focus on other section. You must believe in the power of positivity no matter how tough the situation is. Humour is the best medicine to deal with the stress. Hence, you must try reading or watching some comedy films if stress troubles you. Moreover, you must meet some friends to relax your mind.

(c) **Learn from the Failures:** Success and failures are part of life. There is no successful person who has not tasted failure somewhere. Learning from the failures and giving up, separate the successful and failed people. In other words, the people who focus on learning from mistakes achieve success. The people who become demoralized due to failure can't find success. Thus, your key to success is to learn from the failures. You must assess your work after completing. You must find out the points that seems hinder your progress. It will help you in making compelling plans for the next time you sit to attempt the task. You will get positive results due to believing in the power of positivity.

(d) **Imagine success and forgive yourself:** To meet success, you must have a plan, determination and power of positivity. Imagining success is also a key to success. Moreover, it may also motivate you to achieve your goals. Thus, you must try to visualize what you want to achieve in life. You should imagine your road-map to success. You must imagine the difficulties and ease you may have in the search of success. You may have some regrets about some personal or professional issues. It may freeze you if you try to overcome those regrets. This way it may affect your progress a lot. The ideal thing here is to learn to forgive yourself. In such situation, you must pat yourself on the back and try to overcome the negative thoughts. You must accept your mistakes and tell yourself that everyone makes mistakes. It will prove to be a key to success for you as you will overcome the regrets.

(e) **Stay focused on the present:** You may have worries about some past or future things. This leads you not to give needed focus to the present. Not giving time to the present leads to many mistakes. The result is you find yourself stuck with sorting out mistakes from the past and worrying about the future. Present moment is the best moment to live in. Focusing on the present will help you in taking the right steps in everything. Taking right steps is the key to success and that is what you want ultimately.

(f) **Make positive friends and mentors:** We will also recommend you to stay in the circles that are positive. It will give you positive vibes which are essential to succeed. So, you must try to make friends who have power of positivity. Furthermore, you must have mentors who will help you in learning from your mistakes. They must show you the right path to do a certain thing.

Chapter 3

Preparing yourself for Success: Self-Belief

"Believe you can and you're halfway there."

1. Self-belief is confidence in your own abilities or judgment. It's believing you can do it, believing your deserve it and believing you'll get it. It is one of the most important qualities to have in every aspect of our lives. Whether this is in a personal context or a professional one, belief in oneself is often the difference between success and failure. Yet so many people struggle to find that self-belief, and if that applies to you then don't worry, you're not alone.

2. The biggest difference between successful people and unsuccessful people isn't intelligence or opportunity nor resources. It's the belief that they can make their goals happen. To put yourself on the track to

success, you need to understand that your brain always plays against you. It doesn't care about your big goals, the only thing it wants is to keep you alive. Therefore, we experience procrastination, self-doubt, negative thinking, and anxiety and so on. The sure-fire way to overcome these obstacles is to not believe in them and truly believe in yourself.

3. Honestly, if you don't believe you're going to succeed, then how on Earth would anybody else do? Let's say you want to build a successful business and you need to convince the investors that your idea is the one worth putting funds into. The first thing is to absolutely believe your concept is going to succeed, otherwise no one will have trust in it. You won't either. Imagine living a life without arms and legs. This is the reality of Nick Vujicic. Most people including himself doubted his ability to live a normal life. He even attempted suicide. The moment he found belief, however, it became a turning point. Now, Nick lives a life without limitations, traveling the world and inspiring millions of people to believe in themselves, regardless of their circumstances.

4. The problem with self-belief, and self-confidence, is that there is no 'one fits all' solution. Being able to develop confidence in yourself can depend on a number of factors.

It all depends on what motivates you, what makes you happy, who you look up to, your personal experience and a variety of other factors. What is certain is that self-belief is essential when it comes to success in anything we do in life.

5. **But how do you do that? In** reality there is no 'quick-fix' solution. What's important is that you know self-belief is achievable, and with it everything else becomes more achievable too.

    (a) Review your past and focus on the times you've been successful. Talk about their accomplishments. Try talking to former co-workers who can relate and acknowledge your qualities. Cherish your moments of success however small they are.

    (b) Don't lose hope on encounter with failures. Our greatest glory is in never falling but in rising every time we fall. If you don't believe in yourself, then no one will.

    (c) The chances are that you will not succeed straight away. There will be obstacles, hindrances and mountains of hardships. The most important thing to do is to pursue your goal with perseverance, sheer dedication and moving forward undauntedly.

(d) One of the keys to self-belief is happiness. You need to do things that make you feel happy and things that you can be proud of. Show passion in what you are doing and gain that sense of accomplishment when you complete something. Get rid of that frown and negative attitude and actually smile.

Chapter 4

Preparing yourself for Success: Self-Motivation

"Push yourself, because no one else is going to do it for you"

1. Most self-motivation definitions consider how you can find the ability to do what needs to be done without influence from other people or situations. Self-motivation is to encourage yourself for a continuous progress towards a goal even when it feels challenging. It's turning your 'shoulds' into 'musts'. Think of some of the most successful people you know. Are they the smartest people you've ever met? The wealthiest? Chances are, they're not ☐ but they are the most motivated to succeed. As the one common denominator of all successful people is their hunger to push through their fears. When you have enough hunger, you can

easily learn how to self-motivate to meet the goals you've set your mind and focus on.

2. So, why do so many people find themselves lacking motivation? The strength to learn how to self-motivate all comes down to your psychology. First, you have to clearly know what it is you want. Think of the reason why you want to succeed and turn to this when things seem tough and you need help with self-motivation.

3. Then, you need to assess the emotion and meaning you're attaching to your successes and failures. When you face a setback, do you tell yourself you're not good enough to succeed? If so, it's time to seriously change your psychology. If you want to have self-motivation, you need to be in the mindset that you're already motivated. When it's time to self-motivate, think of the positive state you want to be in to get things done. How does your body feel when you're motivated? Where are your energy levels? What messages are you conveying with your body language? By tapping into the positive state that you associate with self-motivation, you'll be able to self-motivate more easily and often.

4. **Self-Motivation Techniques.** When you're trying to motivate yourself, appreciate the

fact that you're even thinking about making a change.

(a) **Self-Belief:** Believing in yourself is the first step towards self-motivation. It's only you who will be holding onto yourself when everything else seems to be devastated. Believe yourself. You are your best inspiration. You are the only one who has to either move forward or hold yourself back.

(b) **Goal Setting and Planning:** Goal setting is the major step of motivating oneself, while setting goals individuals must check it initially and before implementing the ideas to make it real. In order to realize dreams, goals must be measurable, tangible, attainable, flexible, specific and realistic. Once goals are set, then proper planning maximizes the chances of success to achieve the goal. Predicting future in advance and preparing various steps to attain the goals can help in eliminating uncertainty.

(c) **Time Management:** Organizing your time is the best way to avoid last minute stress and guilt, stay motivated and set aside quality time for leisure, friends and family. By writing up a weekly plan, you'll keep yourself ahead of approaching deadlines and counteract the feeling that you don't have any pressing work to be done.

(d) **Improve Knowledge and Skills:** Improving knowledge and skills maximizes confidence levels and acts as a boost to the self-motivation nature. Knowledge and skills related to the goals and ideas activate the individual's creativity and innovativeness.

(e) **Self–Awareness:** Knowing one's own strengths and weaknesses enables them to know their hidden talents and at the same time, it gives a chance to rectify the errors and mistakes. Knowing his/her own strengths awakens the self-motivating nature and can make them think in a unique way by finding opportunities to fulfill their goals and desires.

(f) **Look to the success of others:** Turning to inspirational quotes for motivation or looking towards a mentor for advice can help you on your path to success. Read more about famous role models or leaders you look up to and see how they utilize self-motivation. You may be able to pick up some techniques or gain some inspiration as you read about their strategies and struggles.

(g) **Get Moving**: Self-motivation becomes much easier when you're already in motion. It doesn't matter whether you are figuring out how to self-motivate toward working out, tackling your tasks at work or preparing for that big presentation; the more you move, the more energy you will have.

(h) **Positive Attitude:** It can be very difficult to learn how to self-motivate when you get caught up with negativity. Focus on gratitude and adopt an abundance mindset. Be thankful for all the good things in your life and steer your focus from all the things you wish you had. Stop comparing yourself to others and understand that life is happening for you, not to you. The more you look at everything good in your life, the more of it you will attract and the easier it will be to self-motivate to attract even more.

The Challenges of Self-Motivation

5. Self-motivation is often difficult because it comes from you. If you don't take care of the underlying issues that keep you from making progress, you can fall back on blaming others for your failure. In some cases, you can rely

on external factors and friends for motivation, but at the end of the day, you're the one who has to put in the work. By digging deep and learning more about yourself, what holds you back and what drives you forward you can clear the path to progress. By learning early on how to self-motivate and stay on track, you'll ultimately experience greater successes sooner.

Chapter 5

Preparing yourself for Success: Physical Fitness

"Those who think they have not time for bodily exercise will sooner or later have to find time for illness."

1. Technically, exercise causes the release of endorphins, which relieve pain and stress, strengthen the immune system and improves mood, in addition to other effects. Exercise also causes the release of serotonin, often referred to as the "happiness" chemical, which affects humans' moods in a profound way.

2. Physical fitness is essential to our overall health and well-being. The remunerations of regular exercise are both tangible and intangible. Physical benefits from exercise are increased energy levels, builds up the immune system, maintains a healthy weight, and have

a strong fit body. But most importantly the intangible benefits like tamed stress levels, increased mental toughness, improved self-discipline, improved mood, the momentum of accomplishment and positive attitude. When you exercise regularly, you create a peak physical and mental state that positively affects all areas of your life. Physical fitness also allows you to do things that you may not otherwise be able to do so.

3.   As per research nearly all of the successful executives and leaders of the world described physical fitness as a top priority. They exerted that a proper training program will help you to have a better posture, exude more energy, and prepare you to handle the demands of a busy professional life. Without energy you'll look and sound like a dud. The executive who exercises regularly looks and feels energized. They radiate passion, vitality, and energy. Regular exercise is important for maintaining high energy as it relates to leaders' appearances, but it may also be a large determinant in executives' *ability* to lead.

4.   Today in this corporate age physical fitness is a substantial influencer of professional success. It is an undeniable fact that good physical fitness is critical for success at all the levels and being overweight is a serious career

impediment. Today, companies are requiring their executives to go through leadership and management training that includes intense physical exercise. According to *Fortune*, Deloitte has implemented a training program for top executives in which they are required to wake up early in wee hours and workout before beginning the leadership training program. Group training workouts in particular cultivates strong leaders.

5. Regular exercise, in addition to its team building skills, gives executives the ability to maintain high-energy levels through the demands of their jobs, including working long hours and frequent travels. A good leader earns respect for his or her ability to manage employees and achieve the organization's mission, but a great leader also sets an example that health and wellness are always top of the mind.

6. Meditation is an extremely scientific and effective method for stress relief, anxiety and a healthier body. Yoga is simple and easy to practice yet potent tools to enhance health, peace, love, success and inner exploration which help one to cope with the hectic pace of modern life and realize your full potential in all spheres of life. It is a matter of fact that Yoga helps you cut through the struggle

and walk you through life with ease. Yoga provides relief from chronic ailments such as asthma, diabetes, hypertension, obesity, and sleep disorders etc. You will find your body to be more rested and alert than ever before. You may also feel that your productivity, concentration and memory are improving.

7.   Wake up and go to work on yourself before you go to work for anyone else. What we face may look insurmountable, but we are always stronger than we know. Your body can stand almost anything; it's your mind that you have to convince.

Chapter 6

Preparing yourself for Success: Follow Your Inner Voice

"Don't let the noise of others' opinion drown out your inner voice"

1. 'Inner voice' also known as 'Intuition', 'Gut', 'Insight', 'Innate wisdom' 'Soul' etc , can be described as "the ability to understand something immediately, without the need for conscious reasoning". However, our brain unconsciously collects plethora of information through all our senses at all times and processes it at an incredible speed. So that intuition, gut, inner voice comes from masses of information we can't even cognitively or consciously process. Studies from numerous cognitive neuroscientists show that 95% of our brain activity happens at an unconscious

level and only 5% of our cognitive activity (decisions, emotions, actions, behavior) comes from our conscious mind. We absorb information through all our senses all the time and process it at an incredible speed. So that intuition, hunch, inkling, sense, voice, is coming from masses of information we can't even cognitively or consciously process.

2. Then there's cognition; "The mental action or process of acquiring knowledge and understanding through thought, experience, and the senses." This is the logical, thinking part of our mind. Weighing pros and cons; coming to rational conclusions based on data or other factors. These are the voices of reason which often try to override our instincts.

3. There are enough examples around us to prove that whether you call it a hunch, a gut reaction, just a feeling or intuition, inner voice is real and if can be harnessed to increase your ability to influence and transit charisma. Intuition helps you read and understand people in an instant. As explained earlier, inner voice is a combination of your feelings, your wisdom, and your experience. People who are able to distinguish between random thoughts and inner voice are more successful in life and in business.

4. CEOs of large corporations, for example, have access to all the research they need to make sound educated decisions. Yet the successful ones will admit that ultimately they have to follow their heart and use personal intuition. When we pay attention to our instincts, we have the ability to read people from facial expressions, gestures, or tone of voice. This ability comes from our early programming as humans to be able to meet others and instantly decide whether they are friend or foe.

Inner Voice: A Skill One Can Learn and Master

5. Those with the ability to follow their inner voice correctly were able to sense danger or make a new friend. Nowadays, when we meet someone, we usually have categorized them within the first 30 seconds. We have decided whether we like or dislike the person; this judgment comes from our inner voice.

6. However, importance of research cannot be disregarded. One must continuously gather and analyze information. But at some point a decision has to be taken, and then let your inner voice guide you. This will take a little faith and a little practice. Stretch yourself little. Don't let the facts or the opinions of other people put barrier on you. You have to

learn to follow your heart and tap into your priceless inner voice.

7. Some of us are afraid to follow our inner voice because it is so hard to explain. Let me assure you that successful people use it every day. They don't always openly talk about it, but they are using it because inner voice is more valuable than you realize.

8. They use it to enhance their creativity, charisma, and ability to connect with others. Sure, super analytical people tend to shoot down intuition as "woo-woo" concept or just a myth, but it is a skill you can learn and master. Not understanding how something works does not mean that it doesn't work.

9. Inner voice expands our ability to tap into our previous experience, our knowledge, and our stored memories. We might not remember what memories or experience we are drawing on, but something we already have learned is expressed as a gut feeling.

What Blocks Us From Following Our Inner Voice?

10. The main obstacle that blocks us from following our inner voice is convincing ourselves that it works and that it should be taken seriously. It might manifest as an

impulse, an urge, or even an inner voice. We are always receiving information through our inner voice. We just need to listen. How does your inner voice talk to you? What are you listening for? Start listening; and you will save yourself a lot of time, energy, and money.

11. Our inner voice can evaluate our previous experiences, sense the emotions of the moment, and rely on past knowledge. As you practice using your intuition, new and inspiring ideas will instinctively arise on their own. You will be able to solve problems faster. Learn to focus and concentrate; this type of focus will nurture and augment your new found inner strength and inner voice. Your logical mind will fight you on these new thoughts and ideas, but eventually your inner voice will win.

12. Thoughts also diminish your ability to listen to your inner voice. Part of harnessing your inner voice is your ability to control your thoughts.

13. Highly influential and charismatic people have mastered the ability to control and direct their thoughts. They have the ability to focus more on positive thoughts than on negative ones. Finding your inner voice and your intuition

gives you the courage, the confidence, and the insight to do or face anything.

A Link between Success and Sound, Quick Decisions

14. Take a realistic look at your life right now. Are you where you wanted to be? Where you are, is the sum total of your thoughts over the course of a lifetime. Your thoughts program your subconscious mind, which helps you to use your inner voice. Control of your thoughts might come in an instant, or it might take a few days, weeks, or even longer.

15. Nevertheless, your subconscious mind will continue working on a solution. Charismatic people work on this mental training every day, while most people ignore the great potential — thinking they've heard it all before.

16. We have all heard about the power of the inner voice. There is a direct correlation between your ability to make sound quick decisions and your success. Our blind spot is that we second guess ourselves or that we don't even try to listen to our instincts.

17. The first challenge is that perhaps we have tried listening to our inner voice a few times, but it did not work for us; so we become a little nervous and apprehensive. Because it

didn't work once, we think that it will never work. The second challenge is that inner voice sounds a little hokey. We ask ourselves, "Can it really be that easy?" Or we think it works for other people, but not for us. Believe me, intuition works and is part of your core foundation of charisma.

18. **Tune into your Inner Voice in four steps.**

    (a) **Take time to be alone with your thoughts:** Clear your mind, and learn to focus on the moment so that external noise and internal dialog don't drown out your inner voice.

    (b) **Watch your attitude:** Attitude comes from your expectations. Learn to expect with confidence that your intuition will lead and guide you to the right decisions.

    (c) **Listen and comply:** When you get that feeling, instinct or impulse, act on it. You might not understand it, but follow the voice and learn how it communicates with you.

    (d) **Practice and perfect:** Learning to master your intuition will take time, energy, and practice. Start with the small things and build up the use of your intuition.

Walt Disney's Instinct and Intuition

19. Walt Disney had a dream to build Disneyland. He had a gut feeling that a unique amusement park based on his company's creations would appeal to both children and adults. Along the way were thousands of reasons to quit and hundreds of people who told him to give up, but he followed his instinct and listened to his inner voice, not to the criticisms of others.

20. Disneyland was a resounding success and led to other Disney amusement parks, such as Disney World. Later on, Disney was driven and inspired to build EPCOT (Experimental Prototype Community of Tomorrow), a park dedicated to International Culture and Technological Innovation. Everyone told him not to do it, reciting the long list of reasons why it was not a good idea (just as people said about Disneyland).

21. But he had the dream, he felt it was the right thing to do, and he had the courage and willpower to pursue it. Disney could have taken the easy route and given in to his critics, but his inner voice told him to keep going — and he did.

22. The easiest way to master inner voice is to choose a time during the day (morning is usually the best) to think about and ponder

your biggest challenges. Learn to listen to your thoughts, follow your instinct, and solve your challenge.

23. As you obtain more experience and learn to listen to your inner voice and trust your instinct, the process will become easier and feel more natural to you. Keep an open mind and practice these skills. Find the process and techniques that work best for you. Learn from the simple answers for which you can receive immediate feedback and know how well the process is working.

Steven Paul Jobs (1955-2011)

Chapter 7

Stay Hungry! Stay Foolish!! – The Story of Apple

**"Have the courage to follow your heart and intuition.
They somehow already know what you truly want to become. Everything else is secondary. "**

– Steven Paul Jobs

The Story of Apple Inc. is story of a visionary and audacious man who was resolute to turn his wildest ideas into reality. It is the story of his grit, self-belief, self-motivation, self-determination, self-conviction, hard work, and finding opportunity in adversities. He turned a deaf ear to others' opinions and listened to his inner voice. This is the story of Steve Jobs who with this passion created Apple Inc., which started from his parent's garage and laid the groundwork for revolutionary innovation in technology.

Steve Jobs was adopted. Since childhood he had flare for electronics and gadgetry. He lacked resources but was never short of will and idea to achieve what was unthinkable. While in high school, he boldly called Hewlett-Packard co-founder and President William Hewlett to ask for parts for a school project. Impressed by Jobs, Hewlett not only gave him the parts, but also offered him a summer internship at Hewlett-Packard. It was there that Jobs met and befriended Steve Wozniak.

Jobs left college and went on a spiritual trip to India. After returning from India he re-joined Wozniak who was working on a prototype computer as a hobby. To Wozniak, it was just a hobby, but the visionary Jobs grasped the marketing potential of such a device and convinced Wozniak to go into business with him. In 1975, the 20-year-old Jobs and Wozniak set up shop in Jobs' parents' garage, dubbed the venture Apple, and began working on the prototype of the Apple I. To generate the $1,350 in capital they used to start Apple, Jobs sold his Volkswagen microbus, and Wozniak sold his Hewlett-Packard calculator.

Although the Apple I sold mainly to hobbyists, generated enough cash to enable Jobs and Wozniak to improve and refine their design. In 1977, they introduced the Apple II the first personal computer with color graphics and a keyboard designed for beginners. The user-friendly Apple II was a tremendous success, ushering in the era of the personal computer. First year sales topped $3 million. Two years later, sales ballooned to $200 million.

Jobs later ventures like Apple-III, the LISA and Macintosh however were not very successful. By 1980, Apple's shine was starting to wear off. In 1984 Jobs introduced the Apple Macintosh, the first PC to feature a graphical-user interface controlled by a mouse. Jobs was stripped of all power and control. He eventually sold his shares of Apple stock and resigned in 1985. Later Jobs launched NeXT Computer Co. Again the NeXT was too expensive to attract enough sales to keep the company afloat. Undeterred, Jobs switched the company's focus from hardware to software. He also began paying more attention to his other business, Pixar Animation Studios, which he had purchased from George Lucas in 1986. After cutting a three picture deal with Disney, Jobs set out to create the first ever computer animated feature film. Four years in the making, "Toy Story" was a certified smash hit when it was released in November 1995. Fueled by this success, Jobs took Pixar public in 1996, and by the end of the first day of trading, his 80 % share of the company was worth $1 billion. After nearly 10 years of struggle, Jobs had finally hit big times. But the best was yet to come.

Within days of Pixar's arrival on the stock market, Apple bought NeXT for $400 million and re-appointed Jobs to Apple's Board of Directors. Next, Jobs installed the G3 PowerPC microprocessor in all Apple computers, making them faster than competing Pentium PCs. He also spearheaded the development of the iMac, a new line of affordable home desktops, which debuted in August 1998 to rave reviews. Under Jobs' guidance, Apple quickly returned to profitability, and by the end of 1998, boasted sales of $5.9 billion.

Against all odds, Steve Jobs pulled the company he founded and loved back from the brink. Apple once again was healthy and churning out the kind of breakthrough products that made the Apple name synonymous with innovation. But Apple's innovations were just getting started. Over the next decade, the company rolled out a series of revolutionary products, including the iPod portable digital audio player in 2001, an online marketplace called the Apple iTunes Store in 2003, the iPhone handset in 2007 and the iPad tablet computer in 2010. The design and functionality of these devices resonated with users worldwide.

Despite his professional successes, Jobs struggled with health issues. In 2003, he was diagnosed with pancreatic cancer. In mid-2004, he had undergone an operation to remove the cancerous tumor from his pancreas. In January 2011, following a liver transplant, Jobs took medical leave of absence from Apple but continued as CEO and was involved in major strategic decisions for the company. Eight months later, on August 24, Apple's Board of Directors announced that Jobs had resigned as CEO and that he would be replaced by COO Tim Cook. Jobs said he would remain with the company as Chairman.

In October 2011, Jobs passed away at the age of 56 due to complications related to pancreatic cancer.

Jobs was a master of dreaming big and he encouraged others to do the same. He inspired millions and forced people to re-examine their lives and their businesses. Here is a man who has shown with realization of self-worth and full potential, harnessed with the right tools, one can achieve unthinkable. The only thing could stop Jobs was himself; his deteriorating health. He once said that sometimes life is going to hit you in the head with a brick. Don't lose faith. Think Different!!!

"Because the people who are crazy enough to think

they can change the world are the ones who do"

Larry Page and Sergey Brin, Founders of Google
The Garage – were it all started

Chapter 8

From the Garage to Googleplex - The Story of Google

"Don't be afraid of failure. The more you stumble around, the more likely you are to stumble across something valuable."

- Sergey Brin Co-founder Google

1. In the year 1995, Page and Brin, both Ph.D scholars, met by chance at Stanford University when latter was assigned to show Page around campus. As fate would have it, quite the momentous meeting of the minds. By some accounts, they disagreed about nearly everything during that first meeting, but by the following year they struck a partnership. Working from their dorm rooms, they built a search engine that used links to determine the importance of individual pages on the World Wide Web. They called this search engine Backrub, which went on to become Google,

one of the big four technology companies alongside Amazon, Apple and Microsoft.

2. Over the next few years, Google caught the attention of not only the academic community, but Silicon Valley investors as well. Page and Brin raised about $ 1 million from investors, family, and friend, which officially gave birth to Google Inc. with Page as Chief Executive Officer (CEO). With this investment, the newly incorporated team made the upgrade from the dorms to their first office: a garage in suburban Menlo Park, California, owned by Susan Wojcicki (employee no.16 and now CEO of YouTube). Primitive desktop computers, a ping pong table and bright blue carpet set the scene for those early days and late nights. (The tradition of keeping things colourful continues to this day.) The next year Google received $25 million of venture capital funding and was processing 500,000 queries per day.

3. However, both Page and Brin remained intimately involved in running Google. By 2004 the search engine was being utilized 200 million times a day. On August 19, 2004, Google Inc. issued its Initial Public Offering (IPO), which netted Page more than $3.8 billion. In an acquisition reflecting the company's efforts to expand its services

beyond Internet searches, Google purchased in 2006 the most popular website for user-submitted streaming videos, YouTube, for $1.65 billion in stock. In 2011 Page resumed his duties as Google's CEO. Google was restructured in August 2015 as a subsidiary of the newly created holding company Alphabet Inc., and Page became CEO of Alphabet. Page left that post in December 2019 but continued to serve on Alphabet's Board of Directors.

4. Since the beginning, Page and Brin did things unconventionally: from Google's initial server (made of Lego) to the first 'Doodle' in 1998 (the Burning Man Stick figure, a comical message to Google users that the founders were 'out of office'.). Page and Brin figured out new business rules that make a company successful in the internet century. They figured out that technology is transforming virtually every business sector. All the world's information and media is online. Cloud computing can put a super computer in one's pocket.

5. Further they hired people that can have the biggest impact of all and named them **SMART CREATIVES**. These were the product folks who combined technical knowledge, business expertise, and creativity. Page & Brin believed that when you put today's technology tools

in their hand and give them lot of freedom they can do amazing things, amazingly fast. They gave maximum freedom and speed to the employees unlike other companies who believed in minimizing risk. They understood value of experimentation and the virtue of failure.

6. They learned that the only way for businesses to consistently succeed was to create an environment where the smart creative employees can thrive at scale. Most companies' culture just happens; no one plans it. But it means leaving a critical component of your success to chance. Once established, company culture is very difficult to change.

7. The smart approach was to ponder and define what sort of culture you want at the outset of your company's life. And the best way Page and Brin realized was to ask the smart creatives who formed the core team, the one who knew the gospel and believed in it as much as others did, which went on to become the foundation stone of culture at Google, **'live according to your own slogans'**. Subsequently, they codified the values that would guide the company's actions and decisions; such as **'Work in small teams'** (small enough to be fed by two pizzas – The Jeff Bezos two-pizza team rule) and **keep them crowded** – so that

smart creatives thrive on interacting with each other ', design office to maximize energy and interactions not for isolation and status. The mixture you get when you cram them together is combustible, so a top priority was to keep them crowded. '**Work, eat and live together**. **Messiness is a virtue** – a study shows the creativity-enhancing effects of messy desks: orderliness seemed to encourage a general mind-set for conservatism and tradition and disorder had the effect of stimulating the desire for the unknown. **Don't listen to HiPPOs** (Highest Paid Person's Opinion) and establish meritocracy –when quality of idea matters, not who suggests it. **Rule of Seven** – the Google's organizational design suggests that managers have a minimum of seven direct reports to foster less managerial oversight and more employee freedom and one last organization principle is to **organize the company around the people whose impact is the highest**. They knew that "Just Say No" syndrome will never let innovation and new ideas to see the light of the day. Hence they **established a culture of Yes.**

8. Page and Brin had realized at the very beginning, the ultimate value of having a well-established and well understood company culture. It becomes the basis for everything

you and the company do; it is the safeguard against something going off the rails, because it is the rails.

9. There will be failures, but there will be more cases where people over deliver, and when that happens the bar gets even higher. That is the power of a great culture. It can make each member of the company better. And it can make the company ascendant.

10. The spirit of doing things differently was the mantra at Google. The relentless search for better answers continues to be at the core of everything done at Googleplex. Today, Google makes hundreds of products used by billions of people across the globe, from YouTube and Android to Gmail and, of course, Google Search. Their passion for building technology for everyone has stayed with them – from the dorm room to the garage and to this very day.

11. Finally, it is certain that no business wins forever, it is inevitable. Some would find this chilling. They find it INSPIRING.

**- Obviously everyone wants to be successful,
but I want to be looked back on as being very innovative,
very trusted and ethical and ultimately making a
big difference in the world.**

– Sergey Brin.

Chapter 9

Prepare to Update Yourself – Save Time and Effort

1. We all have heard in our childhood the story of the "Thirsty Crow". But for out benefit let me narrate the story one more time only to learn a new moral from the story this time. Here we go! Once there was a thirsty crow. He was looking for water. At last he saw a water pot. But there was very less water in the pot. Taking stock of the available resources, the crow decided to put some pebbles in the pot to raise the level of water in the pot. Resultantly the water did come up. The crow quenched his thirst and flew away happily.

2. However on analyzing the situation, it appears that while doing this whole exercise, lot of time and effort was put into filling the pot with pebbles to raise the level of water and it is also possible that some amount of water might have been soaked by the pebbles,

hence the crow had to lose some portion of his reward to the environment in the play. The story doesn't end here.

3. The same crow was once again very thirsty and he saw a pot with very little water. As we all know, the crow was very creative and innovative. One again he took stock of the available resources by flying around the nearest human settlement. This time he saw a straw. Bingo!! An idea struck to his creative and innovative mind. He used the straw to suck the water and quenched his thirst in no time and less efforts.

4. In all fairness, both solutions to the same problem are correct, innovative and indeed lifesaving. However, with the passage of time, the crow got himself with updated with the latest developments happening around him and found a better way to do things, hence saving a lot of time and effort.

5. In a rapidly changing world, it becomes essential to keep up pace with latest happenings. Not only do you have to stay updated with the latest technological advancements but on latest trends, social things and culture as well. Those who cannot change their minds cannot change anything.

6. Like all mobiles and computer applications have a regular release updates and patches to upgrade their systems for becoming a cutting edge technology similarly, we need to update ourselves to the competitive world. Delete the unwanted things which come in the path of your success, and install the graceful things that help in reaching your destination. But remember, there is no automatic button for our life. You must do it manually to avoid glitches and performance issues. Try to be better version of yourself every new day. On the contrary, every next level of your life will demand an upgraded version of yourself.

7. Every once in a while, when you attempt something new, you may fail, which is natural. But what is more important is, to pick yourself up from failures and learn from them. Don't be afraid to experiment, don't be afraid to learn from setbacks and use those lessons as a stepping stone for the future.

8. Introspecting on your existing skillset is important in order to judge your strengths and weaknesses. While there are numerous professional courses to learn new skills, it is also a good idea to develop skills which may not be strictly relevant to the current job. This will help in developing a fuller understanding

of how things work and inspire you to develop better relationships.

9. Successful people have the ability to predict trends which allow them to figure out the right commodity to sell to the right set of people and eventually they become trendsetters. 'Indian Cricket League' was utter failure and 'Indian Premiere League' is the most successful thing on the Earth.

10. There is plethora of examples of established products and brands that didn't keep pace with the trend and eventually lost their grounds. Nokia and Motorola brands are examples of mobile manufacturing establishments who enjoyed majority of consumer share and leading brands once, but now one is trying hard to reinvent it and the latter has been acquired by a rival company Lenovo. Just as established products and brands need updating to stay alive and vibrant, you periodically need to refresh or reinvent yourself.

11. 'Orkut', 'Pager', Electronic Typewriter' etc., were the paths to technological advancements in the history mankind which enjoyed unparalleled popularity but short lived since new and revolutionary technologies outshined them. Had these organizations continued

with their outdated products, they would have perished for sure. Even 'Facebook', the hottest commodity was losing its ground once to 'WhatsApp'. The idea of 'WhatsApp' was once rejected by the Facebook. The same 'Facebook' had to acquire the 'WhatsApp' in $21.8 Billion in 2014 which could have been its own Flagship product.

12. One should remember that in this era of 21st century, where everything is changing day by day, the things you know, the knowledge you have ...all is going to get outdated. You must update yourself. It always used to be best to be better at one skill-set but now days it has become necessary to update yourself in order to survive in this world. It's not only limited to your education but it applies to everything. Get adjusted with the way this whole world works. You either update yourself or you don't at all do it. Things we know, the knowledge we have is never going to be enough to survive. That is just 1% of what the world knows. So one should always be in the learning stage where he/she keeps on learning things of interest.

Never be satisfied with the knowledge you possess. That is not enough. It's like reaching Everest from Ganga River. It's not going to be easy. Don't waste your tiny little time that at the end of the day sums up to 2-3 hours of wastage. Use it to update yourself....

"Update yourself before the world outdates you"

Chapter 10

Survival of the Fittest

"It's not the strongest of the species that survives, nor the most intelligent but the one most responsive to the change"

- Charles Darwin

1. Staying successful in today's dynamic and constantly evolving world poses a constant demand on skills and willingness to adapt to change. To adapt is to be the right "thing" at the right time, where that "thing" may be a product or service, price, convenience, conversation, a physical presence, verbal tone or non-verbal communiqué that emits the solution you want to convey.

2. Companies don't fail because of changes in the environment; they fail because their leaders are either unwilling or incapable of dealing with the said change. In fact, companies don't change. People do. Which means that

to stay competitive in today's environment it demands not only the skill and will to adapt to change but also the foresight to anticipate it.

3. However, there's a misconception about adaptability in that to adapt you must alter who you are at your core, which simply isn't true. Adapting to change is what keeps us relevant, valuable and at the forefront of the competitive edge. It's a leadership choice to remain current, but doing so doesn't change who you are at your core. Just think of a chameleon. To survive in the lizard world, chameleons must change colors but doing so doesn't change the fact that they're still little green lizards.

4. Consider this. Of the companies listed on the Fortune 500 in 1955, only 61 (or 12%) remained in 2014. That means 88% of the original companies either went bankrupt, merged, or fell from grace due to decreased total revenues. Less than 1 % of companies actually make the Fortune 500 list, which means those that do are the best at what they do. In fact, 50 years ago, the life expectancy of a firm in the Fortune 500 list was around 75 years. Today, it's less than 15 years and declining.

5. Unfortunately, one of the reasons companies plummet isn't because they fail to strive for *better*, but because they don't ask themselves the right questions and/or are unwilling to implement the solution. As a result, they don't evolve. Just ask any of the companies below how important adaptability is.

6. In today's mobile fast world where unexpected change is the flavor of the day (every day), organizations need to adapt at the intersection of learning and leadership; they must compete at the speed of adaptability and adapt at the speed of learning. You can only adapt at the rate at which you learn that what was once held to be true, no longer is. But knowledge without application is worthless☐it's about as valuable as yesterday's news which speaks about the importance of a leader's willingness to enter the unknown and pave the new pathways.

7. To survive change, constantly adapt to change. Here are four ways to do so:

    (a) **Learn to Manage Unexpected / Uncertain:** To manage unexpected and uncertain things we need to have full control over our life or business etc. We should constantly cultivate our skill sets and knowledge exponentially to master the craft. Our operations shouldn't be depended on any other factor which is under the control of some third party. Calm and patient attitude just like MS Dhoni can provide right perspective to handle any difficult unseen situation.

(b) **Fuel Curiosity:** Curiosity arises when there's a gap between what you know and what you need to know to be effective and to fuel curiosity is to keep people engaged. The bottom line is this: knowledge feeds knowledge. When you know more you want to learn more; you want to learn how the information at hand supports your endeavor.

(c) **Harness Technology:** Arm yourself with the right information by harnessing technology. Technologically challenged person can never adapt to change.

(d) **Clear Vision:** When people are aware of their goal, they can easily choose their path and move forward by capitalizing their skill and knowledge.

(e) The art of life is a constant readjustment to our surroundings. The key to success is often ability to adapt. The pessimist complains about the wind. The optimist expects it to change. But leader adjusts the sails. People will try to tell you that all the great opportunities have been snapped up. In reality, the world changes every second, blowing new opportunities in all directions, including yours. Life happens. Adapt. Embrace change, and make the most of everything that comes your way.

"Change is the only constant in life. One's ability to adapt to those changes will determine your success in life." - Benjamin Franklin

Chapter 11

Be Balanced in Approach

**"Life is like riding bicycle.
To keep your balance, you must keep moving. "**

1. The best and safest thing is to keep a balance in your life, acknowledge the great powers around us and in us. If you can do that, and live that way, you are really a wise man. Be kind, but don't let people abuse you. Trust, but don't be deceived. Be content, but never stop improving yourself. Life should be a balance between maturity and happiness otherwise, you would never live your life under the pressure of maturity. The foundation stones for a balanced success are honesty, character, integrity, faith, love and loyalty.

2. Awareness is the power working as a 'Weighing Balance' in our lives always measuring the intensity of everything by applying the weights and measures provided by our mind

and intellect and is in every way working in us. Now this depends on us as to what we are going to hear, consider and give effect to. Because the biggest hurdle in our lives is a heart full of lust and desires in life. It is then left to our mind and the efforts made by it to provide the outlets for such lust. Here also our awareness shall guide us by weighing each and every event and the resultant requirement of our heart and body, so as to let us know that what is wrong and what is right for us. At times we retrace our steps from the extreme verge of anything only because of the faculty of awareness which works properly and tell us that the path adopted by us in not the right track and that we should not proceed. Everything so revealed and expressed by our awareness will more often than not, be the correct decision. The only question that remains is that of hearing and appreciating such inner voice of awareness. It all depends on the self-ability of each person to exercise such option because this principle does not apply to one and all. It is more dependent on the family background and other social environment of the person besides his education, upbringing, and experience gained through life and travelling far and wide and upon facing different situations in life which enhance one's awareness.

Life and its responsibilities are the two wheels of a vehicle. These can only move together and neither single one of them are independent of each other. The way in which we cannot move any vehicle on one wheel, similarly, no life can move forward without squarely meeting all its responsibilities. This principle has been proven in history and we are guided by this principle through generations. This, in other words, is a natural phenomenon which comes into a being even at the time of birth and lives with him. We can always observe that whatever we do in our lives is merely the fulfillment of such responsibilities in life, such as marrying while in youth, then bringing up the family and seeking the completion of their educational or vocational training for further settlement in life and then completing the circle by performing their marriage and so on and so forth.

The most important factor is that all of us are chained into this circle and fulfilling our responsibilities in such a manner that it can never be left alone. The way we do not wish to send our children away, similarly our parents would have thought of the same. All those moments are always full of agony and it hurt when we are parting away from our children, near and dear ones. The same feeling is there when our children part company to build a family of their own and leave behind their parents or elders who had devoted all their like time, money, energy and effort to raise them to such present position. Leaving behind such persons, who have helped us in reaching these heights, show nothing short of our ungratefulness. However, if we give the entire situation a little bit more attention, we can always work out situations to the benefit of all concerned.

For this purpose, we must have a cool and balanced mind and give respect, love and affection to our parents and elders. They have a revered position in our lives similar to the expectations we have from our own children. Moments will come in our lives when we do not have the considerations of importance for a particular group of people meaning our parents and elders while treating our spouse and children in an entirely different light and completely forget all and everything that our elders have done for us.

There are only two occasions in life which we cannot get rid of. One is our past which relates to our parents, brothers, sisters, and other is the future, where we have to deal with our spouse and children. Both these situations are an important and integral part of our lives for which we should create such an atmosphere where only happiness and peace should prevail and we should not be faced with any pessimism. All this is possible only through intelligence, concentration and the balancing act in all the given situations. However, we must not forget that this aspect in life is definitely achievable but requires utmost devotion and the will to do so.

"Balance never let success go to your head, and never let failure go to your heart."

**Being challenged in life is inevitable,
Being defeated is optional.**

– Roger Crawford

Chapter 12

Manage Every Challenging Situation

"When faced with a challenge, look for a way, not a way out." - David Weatherford

1. Henry Ford once said "Most people spend more time and energy going around problems than in trying to solve them." Challenges are what makes life interesting and overcoming them is what makes life meaningful.

2. In all aspects of life, we will come across numerous difficult situations to deal with from time to time. These difficult situations might include personal health, declining business, and deteriorating individual or team performance, trying to improve a doomed establishment, a process that it is not working, staff or other resource shortages or adverse media coverage etc.

3.   Is there a template solution that is going to work every trying situation which can guarantee success? Probably not! However, there are some ways to effectively deal with those difficult or challenging situations during leadership and management.

   (a)   **Analyse the Issues at Hand:** First step to successful resolution of challenges would be to establish facts. Try to establish all the facts and figures, join dots and get the correct picture of the solution. Calmly analyse the situation. Don't work on hearsays. Be alert to being swayed by the opinions of those who are strong characters. When people make claims or assertions, ask for specific examples of what happened and when it happened. Often you find that there isn't a lot of substance behind what is being said.

   (b)   **Find out the Core Issues by asking the right questions:** Try to reach to the core issues by asking WHEN, HOW, WHAT, WHERE variety of questions, Think of it as like peeling an onion, each layer is getting you closer to the core. Open questions are much better way of getting to the core of the issue like (i) When did this issue arise? (ii) How did it impact on what you were trying to achieve? (iii) What would be an ideal outcome from your perspective? (iv) What options are there? (v) How can we move forward? Etc.

(c) **Active listening**: There is little point in asking great questions if you are not actively listening to what is being said. Consider all the different points of view. Better listening leads to better understanding and a better response in my experience.

(d) **Avoid Prejudices:** Don't jump the gun. We all tend to draw conclusions at the very beginning. While these might be right at the end of the day, don't let prejudices get in the way of establishing the real issues. Try to remain open minded and objective rather than assuming or guessing.

(e) **Act Professionally:** Try to be as professional as possible in your dealings during challenging times. Don't let emotions takeover your psych. Go by the books. Think about the longer term consequences instead of immediate unethical short term solutions. People will respect you more and your credibility will be boosted by proving your mettle during difficult times.

(f) **Negotiation Skills:** It is not always possible that you will find perfect solutions. It may require some careful negotiation skills to constitute a good outcome to satisfy all the aspects of issues at hand.

(g) **Remember there is no one size fits all approach:** Each situation is different. While there might be some common ground, remember there is unlikely to a one size fits all approach to difficult situations. Adapt your approach depending on the situation.

4. Good planning and preparation will help make sure that you are able to adapt while dealing with the situation or issue. Bottom Line – Handling difficult situations is just a part and parcel of managing and leading. Focus on developing your competence.

Chapter 13

Be Interactive

**"We human beings thrive on interaction.
So just by simply talking to someone you can
expand your individual body of knowledge and
exponentially
increase your collective power"**

1. As per Merriam-Webster Dictionary, definition of **Interactive** is mutually or reciprocally active, involving the actions or inputs of a user especially of, relating to, or being a two-way electronic communication system (such as a telephone, cable television, or a computer) that involves a user's orders (as for information or merchandise) or responses (as to a poll) or in simple words "requiring people to talk with each other or do things together." It is designed to be used in a way that involves the frequent participation of all involved.

2. An interactive personality, which involves a two way communication, wherein being a good speaker and even better listener will not only break ice but also can open tough bottle necks is challenging situations. Organizations today are incorporating interactive training into their learning and development strategies. Interactive training has proven to be more effective in terms of delivering quality output. Interaction with environment helps in retaining attention span, information retention, real time feedback, improves problem solving skills, team building and increases motivation.

3. In any sector, work isn't just about cashing a pay cheque at the end of the month. It's about meeting likeminded people, sharing ideas and working towards a common goal. Being in the same room as a client or colleague, shaking hands with them or simply having coffee with a new potential business partner gives you an accurate understanding of a situation without having to guess what is meant by digital correspondence. It offers us the chance to pick up gestures, tone and nuance which are things that over email may be misinterpreted. Human interaction remains a vital component of customer satisfaction, even in the 'digital age'.

4. Today in this digital age, we can use technology to facilitate, not replace human interactions. Social Networking sites are fantastic tools but a relationship based on electronic communications is one doomed to fail. Prioritize human interaction in both your professional and personal life. Make time regularly in your calendar for meetings but also for informal lunches and coffees. It is often at the relaxed and informal meet ups where we learn the most.

5. Everyone aspires to be the most interesting person in the room. We want our personality to be so charming that we could just influence others. But we find it difficult to interact with people we meet for the very first time. There has been many an occasions where we have found ourselves in a room full of people we don't know, trying to build up the courage to start a conversation with a complete stranger.

6. When you find yourself having to speak to people you haven't met before you can experience feeling shy and unsure how to break the ice or maybe you feel lost for words and wondering what to say.

These are the tips to help make your interactions more effective:

(a) **Keep a Smiling Face:** This sounds very simplistic but if you get used to smiling at everyone you come into contact with, it makes you appear so much more welcoming and open to engage in conversation. If you smile at the people you meet, it is much more likely that they will start chatting with you.

(b) **Eye Contact:** If you feel shy around new people, you may find yourself avoiding eye contact. It can feel too intense and a bit intimidating. Looking someone in the eyes makes you appear more friendly, and confident. It helps you understand what the other person is thinking and feeling. It also ensures you are putting your focus on the other person, which means you come across as more engaging.

(c) **Display Positive Body Language:** Notice your body language. Do you appear welcoming? Do you look like you are open to being approached and for people to start a conversation or are you closed off to any interactions with others? The more positive and open body language you display the more you will attract others to initiate a conversation with you.

(d) **Make Observations:** In order to make the first move when interacting with new people, try making an observation about the situation you are currently in. You can comment on whether it is busy or quiet, the weather, the music, and beauty of the place you are located, literally anything you can think of that will break the ice. This can be a really good conversation starter.

(e) **Ask Great Questions:** Most people love to talk about themselves. Have a list of great questions up your sleeves that you can ask, to find out more about them and to get a conversation started. Make it all about them. Ask open-ended questions to find out as much as you can about the other person, encouraging them to talk at length as opposed to being limited by a shorter answer.

(f) **Listen Intently:** We often listen with intention rather than actively listening. We might listen with the intention to ask the next question or to give our view on what is being said. Try listening with such deep interest that you have no other motive than to purely just hear what the other person is saying. Let them carry on speaking until they have completely finished what is on their mind. Great listening skills take some practice to master, but once you are a great listener it will make you much better equipped to interact with others, as people love feeling listened to.

(g) **Embrace Rejection:** The feeling of being rejected is one of the worst feelings we can experience. If we feel that our presence is not wanted or we are not welcome, it can cause us to feel hurt. When the rejection is from a stranger that we have only just met, there are a couple of ways to deal with it. The first is to conclude that it isn't personal. Most people are happy meeting new people, but some aren't, we can't change that, we can just accept it. The second is to learn from it. Not every interaction we have with a new person will go well. Don't sweat it if it doesn't, just identify what went wrong and keep practicing.

www.ingramcontent.com/pod-product-compliance
Lightning Source LLC
Chambersburg PA
CBHW020742160726
47993CB00006B/2576